Johann Sebastian Bach

Brandenburg Concertos Nos. 4–6

BWV 1049–1051

Edited by Roger Fiske (no. 4) and Karin Stöckl (nos. 5–6)

Urtext

EULENBURG

Contents / Inhalt

EAS 103
ISBN 3-7957-6503-X
ISMN M-2002-2337-8

Urtext editions based on Eulenburg Study Scores ETP 281, 282 and 255
Preface by Ulrike Brenning taken from *Lexikon Orchestermusik Barock*, ed. Wulf Konold and Eva Reisinger,

Brandenburg Concerto No. 5

Brandenburg Concerto No. 6

Preface

From August 1717 to April 1723 Johann Sebastian Bach was Kapellmeister and Master of the Royal Chamber Music at the Court of Prince Leopold of Anhalt-Cöthen. Bach expressed his feelings about this post retrospectively in a letter to his long-standing friend Georg Erdmann, written in 1730. One may gather from this letter that for Bach the well-paid post of Kapellmeister obviously carried with it a certain prestige and for that reason he felt it to be a demotion to have to trouble himself with a choirmaster's job. On the other hand Bach's comments make it clear that the working conditions in Cöthen became increasingly difficult with the approaching marriage of Leopold to Friederica Henrietta von Bernburg, which took place at the end of 1721. Bach had in fact, in November 1720, already tried to make a change by applying – though without success – for the vacant post of choirmaster at the Jakobikirche in Hamburg.

In this context the fact that Bach sent selected concertos to Berlin, in a dedicatory manuscript, beautifully prepared as a fair copy in his own hand, for Christian Ludwig, Margrave of Brandenburg, youngest son of the Electoral Prince, has particular significance. According to the requirements of his secular post, Bach composed almost exclusively keyboard works, chamber music and instrumental concertos during his time at Cöthen. So when he dedicates some of his works to an equally secular master it is natural to suppose that he would choose them from this repertory. Furthermore, in the text of the inscription (in French) to the Margrave dated 24 March 1721, he makes reference to concrete grounds for the dedication of these *Six Concerts avec plusieurs instruments*, named nowadays, after their dedicatee, the 'Brandenburg Concertos': 'A couple of years ago I had the good fortune to be heard by your majesty [...]. Your majesty honoured me with the request that I send you a few of my compositions.'

The circumstances of this performance have been much puzzled over. A coincidental meeting between Bach and the Margrave in Meiningen, of which Christian Ludwig's brother-in-law was Duke, or in Carlsbad during a trip made by Leopold early in 1718 would be possibilities; it is more likely however that Bach met the Margrave in Berlin at the beginning of 1719. Prince Leopold had ordered a harpsichord and instructed Bach to collect the instrument from Berlin – as can be verified from an item for travel expenses in the accounts for 1 March 1719.

The Margrave may well have expressed the desire to hear more of Bach's compositions at the time of this performance. The fact, however, that Bach did not comply with the Margrave's wishes until the sudden dedication of these six concertos two years later makes it much more likely that a secret request was the real reason behind the sending of the scores.

This theory is supported by further observations. As already mentioned, for the enclosures which accompanied this dedicatory manuscript Bach drew on the repertoire of instrumental concertos which he had in all probability composed in and for Cöthen – taking into account, of course, the circumstances in Berlin, with which he must have been familiar both from his journey there and from the lively exchange of musicians which took place between Cöthen and Berlin. He probably hoped to perform the concertos himself in Berlin.

In its six works the score mirrors the whole range of types of concertante ensemble music current at the time: the third and sixth concertos display the characteristics of social music-making most clearly, the second and fourth more the concerto grosso type, and Concertos 1 and 5 in their final autograph form document the development towards the solo concerto. Furthermore, a comparison with the copies, still in existence, of the early versions of Concertos 1, 2 and 3 made by the Bach scholar Christian Friedrich Penzel shortly after Bach's death in Leipzig, and of Concerto No. 5 made by Johann Christoph Altnickol, shows that the diversity of the concerto type was extended in many respects in the writing out of the dedicatory score. Bach enriched the instrumentation by the use of unusual instruments such as the *violino piccolo* in No. 1 and *flauto d'echo* in No. 4; he divided the cello part in No. 3 and expanded the cadenzas of the solo instruments in Concerto No. 5. In addition, the treatment of the sequence of movements shows Bach's desire to display his skills to the full – by choosing a two-movement composition for the third piece and by extending the first concerto in the drawing up of the manuscript to a quasi four-movement piece.

Although Bach provides a representative cross-section of his concertos in the dedicatory score, it would be mistaken to think of them in terms of a cycle. We have here merely a collection of pre-existing concertos composed as individual works.

After the death of Margrave Christian Ludwig the dedicatory manuscript came into possession of the Bach scholar Johann Philipp Kirnberger. He in turn handed the score on to his pupil Princess Amalie of Prussia and it was bequeathed with her library to the Joachimsthalschen Gymnasium. From there the score was finally passed on to the Berlin Staatsbibliothek. It was not published until 1850 when, on the centenary of Bach's death, the Brandenburg Concertos were printed for the first time by C. F. Peters in Leipzig.

Karin Stöckl
Translation: Penny Souster

Brandenburg Concerto No. 4
in G major BWV 1049

Composed: in 1719/1720
Original date of publication: not published during the composer's lifetime
Instrumental ensemble: Solo: violin, flauto (recorder) 1, 2;
Ripieno: violins I and II, viola, cello, violone, continuo
Duration: ca. 14 minutes

The fourth Brandenburg Concerto is markedly different from the 'ensemble concertos' Nos. 1 and 2 in the set; although it was composed very soon after the second concerto, the stylistic differences between the two works are readily apparent. The main stylistic difference lies in the handling of the solo parts: this applies both to the highly idiosyncratic writing of the individual solo parts and the relationship between solo and *tutti* passages.

With the introduction of the main thematic idea at the beginning of the first movement, the individual treatment of the solo parts becomes evident: each of the recorders plays the main theme through once before the *solo* violin enters with new material. The fact that Bach wrote this movement with specific instruments in mind becomes very clear in the solo passage for violin from bar 185 onwards: with florid sequences, double-stopping and arpeggios typical of a violinist's style (and close in style to the solo Sonatas and Partitas of 1720), the leading instrument really becomes a solo performer with orchestral accompaniment.

The structure of the movement also follows the direction taken by the solo parts. By alternating those sections that use the main theme with interludes characterized by contrasting thematic material on the solo violin, the focus moves away from the conventional *tutti/solo* form; further, the recorders and strings are not given the same thematic treatment.

After the very long first movement (with 427 bars it is much longer than the other first movements of the Brandenburg Concertos) comes an *Andante*. At the beginning of this movement a rocking theme is introduced in the solo parts and tutti violin parts, though this gentle 3/4 rhythm is immediately challenged by the hemiolas in the bass line. The solo violin takes up this rhythm and it is used in counterpoint with the two solo recorders. The *tutti* and *solo* sections in this movement are also shorter, often succeeding each other one bar at a time in an echo effect.

The third and final movement, *Presto*, provides a marked contrast to the two preceding movements. Neither the soloists' roles nor the conventions of musical form determine the direction of the work here, as, in a compositional tour-de-force, Bach combines a concerto form with a fugue.

At the end of the five-part fugal exposition (b27) the musical texture is already so dense that only a radical change can make room for anything more: beginning with the three solos parts at bar 41 there is an ingenious combination of fugal and *concertante* writing, with neither form being given preference over the other. The structure of the *concertante* line is derived from the fugal theme, although the fugal voices are never mere accompaniment and each take their turn as equal players. All the parts in succession are brought into this combination until the music breaks out in dissonance (from bb 137 and 205 onwards). Bach brings this entirely atypical final movement to an end with a tutti so loud that the final entry of the fugue theme on the recorders is almost inaudible.

Brandenburg Concerto No. 5
in D major BWV 1050

Composed: in 1720/1721
Original date of publication: not published during the composer's lifetime
Instrumental ensemble: Solo: flute, violin, cembalo;
Ripieno: violin, viola, violoncello violone
Duration: ca. 20 minutes

In this concerto Bach reaches far beyond the compass of the other pieces in the cycle. It is neither a *Gemeinschaftsspielmusik* for convivial music-making, like the sixth Concerto, nor a proper group concerto. The almost revolutionary scope of the composition is revealed most clearly in the first movement, *Allegro*.

The movement begins with the main idea, based upon a chord, played in unison by the solo violin and *tutti* violins. The dense string sound is joined by a new voice from bar 9, where for the first time in the Brandenburg Concerto Bach expressly allocates a part to a transverse flute. The flute introduces a lyrical, singing motif, which contrasts with the main theme and can be heard distinctly throughout the rest of the movement. This first movement might be considered to anticipate the style of the 'singing' *Allegro*.

This opening *Allegro* is innovative in another respect, too, however. The harpsichord entry, initially performing as an equal-ranking player in the concerto, changes radically from bar 154 onwards, when a grand 65-bar final cadenza *solo senza stromenti* transforms this piece into a solo concerto. As early as bar 139 the solo part begins to emerge with virtuoso keyboard runs, while the cadenza itself rises above the status of a virtuoso display of technical skills. The most important motif in the cadenza is the downward-fourth quaver figure originally heard in the flute part, which consistently re-emerges from the semiquaver figures in sequential form, sometimes inverted or as a rhythmic fragment. Towards the end of the cadenza the musical energy is gradually compressed until it erupts in a demisemiquaver passage in which the quaver motif is transformed into a rising and falling demisemiquaver figure on the up-beat.

As no evidence has yet been found of any other work showing such advanced and emancipated treatment of a keyboard instrument, the fifth Brandenburg Concerto earns the status of the first solo concerto ever composed for a keyboard instrument.

The second movement, too, stands apart from other slow movements in the cycle in its expressive character, thematic structure and instrumentation. This movement has the title *affettuoso*: an unusual heading for the period. With no instrumental *tutti* in this movement the flute, violin and harpsichord play together as chamber musicians. The imitative development of the main theme is not merely another exercise in counterpoint, but an expressive and intimate musical dialogue. Here the style is palpably close to that of Bach's chamber music with keyboard *obbligato*, such as the Violin Sonatas (BWV 1014–1019) and the Flute Sonatas (BWV 1030–1032).

The powerful momentum of the first movement, which calls for a weighty and densely written second movement, also makes itself felt in the structure of the third movement, *Allegro*. It is unusual to find such a rich variety of musical ideas used in a final movement. After the introduction of the main theme on the solo instruments it is played *tutti*, which soon leads to a transition into the minor key (b 79 onwards). Over an insistent pedal B on the harpsichord the theme emerges in B minor between the flute and the solo violin, followed by a string *tutti* from bar 87.

The harpsichord is again given special prominence in this movement. There is a remarkable solo section without instrumental accompaniment in bars 163–176 in which Bach works the opening theme into a strict canon. When the rest of the solo and ripieno instruments join in again from bar 177, the harmonies become denser once more in a rapid alternation between minor keys. This section ends in B minor in bar 232 before, abruptly and without warning, the movement concludes with an almost note-for-note repetition of the opening 78 bars.

Brandenburg Concerto No. 6
in B♭ major BWV 1051

Composed: in 1718
Original date of publication: not published during the composer's lifetime
Instrumental ensemble: viola da braccio I and II, viola da gamba I and II, violoncello, violone and cembalo
Duration: ca. 16 minutes

The sixth Brandenburg Concerto was probably the first work in the cycle to be completed, at about the same time as the third concerto in G major.

Bach based the structure of this concerto on the Italian trio setting, with two equal-ranking melodic parts in the foreground: Viola da braccio I and II. These two instruments are accompanied by a consistently deep string sound, which affords this concerto a highly individual character. In the first movement, *Allegro*, especially, Bach plays with the various possible combinations of the lower instruments, shading the deep sound quality in different ways. Violas I and II always play in canon, heard distinctly from the opening theme: the closeness of their entries, only a quaver apart, and the structure of the theme, with its striking tied notes, mean that the two parts complement one another intimately.

In the second movement, *Adagio ma non tanto*, the Gambas rest and the colour of the sound brightens a little as the violas da braccio continue playing with the Basso continuo (violone and harpsichord) and an independent cello part. Once again the violas play in canon – the second viola begins, followed in the fifth bar by the entry of the first viola, a fifth above it – while the cello maintains a steady crotchet line in counterpoint with this canon. Various rhythmic values accumulate over the course of the movement to produce a web of notes ranging from semibreves to continuous lines of quavers, while the solemn 3/2 pulse is maintained with the continuing presence of minims.

Bach also used special rhythmic effects in the third movement, *Allegro*. The merry, seemingly uncomplicated 12/8 rhythm is soon broken up in the third bar by wilful syncopations on the two violas. 'Plain' and syncopated rhythms are set against one another, resulting in an intense fluidity of sound where the parts are dovetailed closely together and with a density that almost contradicts the simplicity of the A-B-A form. Now the violas can be heard against the background of the rest of the ensemble as they play in a higher register – and yet they cannot be described as soloists in the usual sense, as there is not a marked contrast between the *tutti* and *concertino* sections; the sixth Brandenburg Concerto, like the third, is a *Gemeinschaftsspielmusik*, a convivial piece for a group of players.

Ulrike Brenning
Translation: Julia Rushworth

Vorwort

Vom August 1717 bis zum April 1723 war Johann Sebastian Bach am Hofe des Fürsten Leopold von Anhalt-Cöthen als Kapellmeister und Direktor der Fürstlichen Kammermusiken tätig. Über diese Anstellung in Köthen äußerte Bach sich rückblickend in einem Brief an seinen langjährigen Freund Georg Erdmann aus dem Jahre 1730, aus dem zu entnehmen ist, dass für Bach offenbar die gut dotierte Kapellmeisterstelle mit einem gewissen Ansehen verknüpft war und er es daher als Rückstufung empfand, sich um ein Kantorenamt bemühen zu müssen. Andererseits deuten Bachs Äußerungen darauf hin, dass die Arbeitsbedingungen in Köthen durch die bevorstehende Heirat Leopolds mit Friederica Henrietta von Bernburg, die Ende des Jahres 1721 erfolgte, zunehmend problematisch wurden, und tatsächlich hatte Bach sich bereits im November 1720 mit seiner – allerdings erfolglosen – Bewerbung um die vakante Kantorenstelle an St. Jakobi in Hamburg beruflich zu verändern versucht.

In diesem Zusammenhang erhält Bachs Übersendung von ausgesuchten Konzerten nach Berlin an den Markgrafen Christian Ludwig von Brandenburg, den jüngsten Sohn des Großen Kurfürsten, in einem von der Hand des Komponisten selbst in kalligraphischer Reinschrift verfertigten Widmungsautograph besondere Bedeutung. Den Obliegenheiten seiner weltlichen Anstellung gemäß komponierte Bach in der Köthener Zeit fast ausschließlich Klavierwerke, Kammermusik und Instrumentalkonzerte. Wenn er also einem ebenfalls weltlichen Herrn einige seiner Werke dedizierte, so ist es naheliegend, dass er sie aus diesem Repertoire auswählte. Im Widmungstext vom 24. März 1721 an den Markgraf (in französischer Sprache) bezieht sich Bach zudem auf einen konkreten Anlass für die Dedikation dieser *Six Concerts avec plusieurs instruments*, die nach ihrem Widmungsträger die heute geläufige Bezeichnung „Brandenburgische Konzerte" tragen: „Vor ein paar Jahren hatte ich das Glück, mich vor Ihrer Königlichen Hoheit hören zu lassen [...] Eure Köningliche Hoheit beliebte mich mit dem Auftrag zu ehren, Ihr einige meiner Kompositionen zu senden."

Über die Umstände des hier angesprochenen Vorspiels ist viel gerätselt worden. Eine zufällige Begegnung Bachs mit dem Markgrafen in Meiningen, dessen Herzog der Schwager Christian Ludwigs war, oder in Karlsbad anlässlich einer Reise Leopolds im Frühjahr 1718, wäre denkbar, wahrscheinlicher aber ist, dass Bach den Grafen direkt in Berlin Anfang des Jahres 1719 aufsuchte. Fürst Leopold nämlich hatte in Berlin einen Kielflügel bestellt und beorderte Bach zur Abholung des Instrumentes dorthin, was der Posten der Reisespesen auf der Abrechnung vom 1. 3. 1719 belegt.

Wohl mag der Markgraf anlässlich dieses Vorspiels den Wunsch geäußert haben, von Bach weitere Kompositionen zu hören. Der Umstand jedoch, dass Bach erst nach zwei Jahren plötzlich mit der Dedikation dieser sechs Konzerte dem Wunsch des Markgrafen nachkam, deutet viel eher auf eine versteckte Bewerbung als wahren Grund für die Übersendung der Partitur hin.

Diese These lässt sich durch weitere Beobachtungen stützen: Wie bereits erwähnt, schöpfte Bach bei der Anlage seiner Widmungshandschrift aus seinem Repertoire von Instrumental-Konzerten, das er aller Wahrscheinlichkeit nach in und für Köthen komponiert hatte, wobei er natürlich die Berliner Verhältnisse berücksichtigt haben dürfte, die er aufgrund seiner Reise dorthin, aber auch aufgrund des regen Musikeraustausches, der zwischen Köthen und Berlin stattfand, genau gekannt haben muß. Er kann also durchaus gehofft haben, die Konzerte in Berlin selbst einmal aufzuführen.

Die Partitur spiegelt mit ihren sechs Werken die gesamte Palette damals gängiger Typen konzertanter Ensemblemusik: Das 3. und 6. Konzert prägen am ehesten den Charakter von Gemeinschaftsspielmusiken aus, das 2. und 4. mehr den Concerto-grosso-Typus und die Konzerte 1 und 5 dokumentieren in ihrer endgültigen Form im Autograph die Hinwendung zum Solokonzert. Darüber hinaus erweist ein Vergleich mit den noch vorhandenen Abschriften der Frühfassungen der Konzerte 1, 2 und 3 durch den Bach-Schüler Christian Friedrich Penzel, die dieser kurz nach Bachs Tod in Leipzig anfertigte, sowie des 5. Konzertes durch Johann Christoph Altnickol, dass die Vielgestaltigkeit der Konzert-Typen in mancher Hinsicht bei der Niederschrift der Widmungspartitur noch erweitert wurde. So bereicherte Bach die Besetzung durch die Verwendung ungebräuchlicher Instrumente wie des *Violino piccolo* im 1. und des *Flauto d'echo* im 4. Konzert, differenzierte den Cellopart im 3. und erweiterte die Kadenz des Soloinstrumentes im 5. Konzert. Außerdem zeigt die Behandlung der Satzfolge Bachs Intention, sein umfassendes Können zur Schau zu stellen, wenn er als drittes Stück eine zweisätzige Komposition auswählt und für die Erstellung des Autographs das 1. Konzert quasi zur Viersätzigkeit erweitert.

Obwohl Bach mit der Widmungspartitur die Darstellung eines repräsentativen Querschnittes durch sein Konzertschaffen gibt, wäre es verfehlt, von einem Zyklus zu sprechen: Es handelt sich lediglich um eine Sammlung präexistenter und als Einzelwerke komponierter Konzerte.

Das Widmungsautograph gelangte nach dem Tode des Markgrafen Christian Ludwig in den Besitz des Bach-Schülers Johann Philipp Kirnberger. Dieser wiederum übereignete die Partitur seiner Schülerin Prinzessin Amalie von Preußen, mit deren nachgelassener Bibliothek sie dem Joachimthalschen Gymnasium ausgehändigt wurde, von wo sie schließlich in den Besitz der Berliner Staatsbibliothek überging. Erst 1850, zu Bachs 100. Todestag, erschienen die *Brandenburgischen Konzerte* beim Verlag C. F. Peters in Leipzig erstmals im Druck.

Karin Stöckl

Brandenburgisches Konzert Nr. 4
G-Dur BWV 1049

Komponiert: 1719/1720
Originalverlag: zu Lebzeiten des Komponisten nicht gedruckt
Orchesterbesetzung: Soli: 2 Blockflöten – Violine;
Orchester: Violine I und II, Viola, Violoncello, Violone, Cembalo
Spieldauer: etwa 14 Minuten

Von den „Gruppenkonzerten“ Nr. 1 und Nr. 2 hebt sich das vierte Brandenburgische Konzert deutlich ab. Obwohl in enger zeitlicher Nähe zum zweiten Konzert entstanden, haben diese beiden Werke deutlich verschiedene stilistische Prämissen. Das grundlegend neue Merkmal liegt in der kompositorischen Gestaltung der Solostimmen. Dies betrifft sowohl die jeweils sehr individuelle Ausarbeitung der einzelnen Solostimmen als auch das Verhältnis zwischen Solo und Tutti.

Bereits gleich mit der Vorstellung des thematischen Hauptgedankens zu Beginn des ersten Satzes im Duett der beiden Flöten und dem nachfolgenden ersten Einsatz der Solo-Violine (T. 13ff.) tritt die differenzierte solistische Behandlung in den Vordergrund: Jede Flöte trägt den Hauptgedanken einmal vollständig vor, bis die Solo-Violine mit anderem Material einsetzen kann, währenddessen setzen die Flöten ihr begonnenes Duett fort. Dass Bach in diesem Satz geradezu „instrumentenspezifisch“ komponiert hat, wird spätestens beim Solo-Abschnitt der Violine ab T. 185ff. klar: Mit Passagen, Doppelgriffen und violintypischen Arpeggien (man spürt die Nähe zu den Solo-Sonaten und -Partiten von 1720) wird das führende Instrument zum echten Solo-Instrument mit begleitendem Orchester.

Der Formaufbau des Satzes folgt den Intentionen der solistischen Gestaltung. Im Wechsel von Abschnitten, die das Hauptthema verwenden, und Zwischenspielen, die vor allem durch die andere Thematik der Solo-Violine bestimmt werden, tritt die konventionelle Tutti/Solo-Form in den Hintergrund, eine gleiche thematische Behandlung von Bläsern und Streichern ist damit ebenso aufgehoben.

Nach dem sehr langen ersten Satz (mit 427 Takten übersteigt er deutlich die Länge anderer Kopfsätze im Zyklus der Brandenburgischen Konzerte) folgt ein *Andante*. Zu Beginn dieses Satzes wird ein wiegendes Motiv in den Solostimmen und den Geigen des Tutti vorgestellt, die schwingende 3/4-Bewegung jedoch sogleich durch die Hemiolen im Bass irritiert. Davon gleichsam angeregt, greift die Solo-Violine sie auf und kontrapunktiert damit die beiden Solo-Flöten. Tutti- und Solo-Abschnitte sind in diesem Satz kürzer, oft folgen sie als Echowirkung mit Längen von jeweils einem Takt aufeinander.

Der dritte Satz, *Presto*, schafft zu den beiden vorangegangenen Sätzen einen starken Gegensatz. Weder sind es solistische Aufgaben noch eine „gefällige" Form, die hier leitende Ideen bei der Komposition waren. In einer höchst artifiziellen Weise verknüpft Bach in diesem Schlusssatz eine Konzertform mit einer Fugenform.

Am Ende der fünfstimmigen Fugenexposition (T. 27) ist das musikalische Geschehen bereits so dicht, dass nur eine radikale Veränderung neuen Raum schaffen kann: Ab T. 41 beginnt die geniale Verbindung von Fuge und Konzertieren, zunächst nur in den drei Solostimmen, ohne dass dabei der einen oder anderen Form der Vorzug gegeben würde. Die Gestaltung der „konzentierenden" Stimme leitet sich aus dem Material des Fugenthemas ab, die Fugenstimmen sind ihrerseits nie Begleitstimmen, sondern jeweils gleichberechtigte Mit- und Gegenspieler. Sukzessive werden alle Stimmen in diese Verknüpfung eingebunden, bis sich die Musik in Dissonanzbildungen entlädt (T. 137ff. und T. 205ff.). Ein Tutti, in dessen Klangstärke der letzte Einsatz des Fugenthemas der Flöten fast verhallt, beendet diesen so ganz untypischen Schlusssatz.

Brandenburgisches Konzert Nr. 5
D-Dur BWV 1050

Komponiert: 1720/1721
Originalverlag: zu Lebzeiten des Komponisten nicht gedruckt
Orchesterbesetzung: Soli: Flöte – Violine – Cembalo;
Orchester: Violine, Viola, Violone
Spieldauer: etwa 20 Minuten

In diesem Konzert greift Bach weit über die Werkpläne der übrigen Stücke im Zyklus hinaus. Es ist weder eine Gemeinschaftsspielmusik noch ein echtes Gruppenkonzert. Der geradezu revolutionäre Kompositionsentwurf offenbart sich vor allem im ersten Satz, *Allegro*.

Der Satz beginnt mit dem dreiklangsbetonten Hauptgedanken, der *unisono* in der Solo-Violine und den Tutti-Violinen geführt wird. In das dichte Streicherklangbild tritt ab T. 9 ein neuer Klang: Zum ersten Mal schreibt Bach ausdrücklich eine Querflöte in der Partitur eines Brandenburgischen Konzertes vor. Bereits an dem veränderten Klangideal lässt sich ein neuer Werkstil ablesen. Die Flöte setzt dem Hauptgedanken ein lyrisch-gesangliches Motiv entgegen, welches sie im gesamten Satz beibehält und immer deutlich hervortritt. Man könnte in diesem ersten Satz den Typus des „singenden" *Allegro* vorweggenommen sehen.

Innovativ ist das *Allegro* jedoch noch in einer anderen Hinsicht. Der instrumentale Einsatz des Cembalo, zunächst als gleichberechtigt-konzertierendes Instrument verwendet, verändert sich radikal ab T. 154: eine groß angelegte 65taktige Schlusskadenz *solo senza stromenti* verwandelt dieses Konzert in ein Solokonzert. Bereits ab T. 139 wird die Solopassage in virtuosen klavieristischen Läufen vorbereitet. Die Kadenz selbst übersteigt den Status einer virtuosen Vorführung von technischen Raffinessen. Das wichtigste Motiv ist die abwärts führende Achtel-Figur der Querflöte, die einen Quartfall markiert. In sequenzierter Form tritt es aus den Sechzehntel-Figuren immer wieder hervor, wird umgekehrt oder als rhythmische Floskel beibehalten. Zum Ende der Kadenz hin werden Energien gestaut und entladen sich in Zweiunddreißigstel-Passagen, in denen das Achtel-Motiv der Flöte als auftaktige Zweiunddreißigstel-Figur auf- bzw. untergeht.

Solange kein anderes Werk nachgewiesen werden kann, welches vor 1720 entstand und eine ähnlich avancierte und emanzipierte Behandlung des Tasteninstruments aufweist, hat das fünfte Brandenburgische Konzert den Status des ersten Solokonzertes für ein Tasteninstrument in der Musikgeschichte inne.

Auch der zweite Satz fällt im Ausdruck, in der thematischen Gestaltung sowie in der Instrumentierung aus der Gruppe der langsamen Mittelsätze des Zyklus heraus. Der Satz ist überschrieben mit *affettuoso*, eine für die damalige Zeit ungewöhnliche Satzüberschrift. Durchgehend ohne Orchester-Tutti musizieren Querflöte, Violine und Cembalo (vielleicht hatte Bach bei der klanglichen Konzeption auch an einen Kielflügel gedacht) kammermusikalisch miteinander. Die imitierende Verarbeitung des Hauptgedankens ist nicht nur mehr Kontrapunktik, sondern ein ausdrucksstarker kammermusikalischer Dialog. Hier wird die stilistische Nähe zu Bachs Kammermusik mit obligatem Clavier, z. B. den Sonaten für Violine (BWV 1014–1019) und den Sonaten für Querflöte (BWV 1030–1032) spürbar.

Der stark bewegte erste Satz, der einen gewichtigen und dichten zweiten Satz fast nach sich ziehen musste, wirkt sich auch noch auf die Gestaltung des dritten Satzes, *Allegro*, aus. Ungewöhnlich für die Gestaltung eines letzten Satzes ist der vielfältige Wechsel der musikalischen Einfälle. Nach der Einführung des Hauptthemas in den Solo-Instrumenten wird es vom Tutti aufgenommen, das bald einen Wechsel nach Moll herbeiführt (T. 79ff.). Über einem insistierenden Orgelpunkt h im Cembalo entfaltet sich das Thema in h-Moll zwischen Querflöte und Solo-Violine, das Streichertutti folgt ab T. 87.

Auch dieser Satz räumt dem Cembalo eine besondere Bedeutung ein. Auffällig ist z. B. der Soloteil ohne Orchester T. 163–176: Hier verarbeitet Bach das Kopfthema in einem strengen Kanon. Wenn anschließend die übrigen Solo- und Tutti-Instrumente ab T. 177 wieder hinzutreten, kommt es nochmals zu einer Verdichtung der Harmonik in schnellen Wechseln von Molltonarten. Dieser Teil schließt in T. 232 auf h-Moll ab; abrupt und unvermittelt erklingt dann ab T. 233 die quasi notengetreue Wiederholung der Takte 1–78.

Brandenburgisches Konzert Nr. 6
B-Dur BWV 1051

Komponiert: 1718
Originalverlag: zu Lebzeiten des Komponisten nicht gedruckt
Orchesterbesetzung: Viola da braccio I und II, Viola da gamba I und II, Violoncello, Violone und Cembalo
Spieldauer: etwa 16 Minuten

Das 6. Brandenburgische Konzert ist wahrscheinlich das erste Werk des Zyklus', entstanden in zeitlicher Nähe zum 3. Konzert in G-Dur.

Bach nahm sich bei der Gestaltung dieses Konzerts den italienischen Triosatz zum Vorbild und stellte demzufolge zwei gleiche Melodiestimmen in den Vordergrund: Viola da braccio I und II. Diese beiden Instrumente werden umgeben von einem durchweg tiefen Streicherklang, der dem Konzert einen sehr eigenen Charakter verleiht. Vor allem der erste Satz, *Allegro*, spielt mit den verschiedenen Kombinationen der tiefen Instrumente, so dass die tiefe Klangfarbe verschiedene Schattierungen erhält. Viola I und II befinden sich in einem ständigen Kanon, der sich bereits im Hauptthema deutlich vernehmen lässt: Der enge zeitliche Einsatzabstand von nur einer Achtelnote und die Struktur des Themas mit den auffälligen Überbindungen sorgt für eine komplementäre Ergänzung der beiden Stimmen.

Im zweiten Satz, *Adagio ma non tanto*, hellt sich durch das Pausieren der Gamben die Klangfarbe etwas auf, lediglich die Bratschen musizieren mit dem Basso continuo (Violone und Cembalo) und einer eigenständigen Cellostimme. Auch in diesem Satz stehen die Bratschen in einem Kanonverhältnis zueinander: Die zweite Bratsche beginnt, gefolgt im fünften Takt vom Einsatz der ersten Bratsche in der Oberquinte. Das Cello kontrapunktiert diesen Kanon mit einer in Vierteln dahinschreitenden Linie. Die rhythmischen Werte verdichten sich im Verlauf des Satzes und es entsteht ein Gewebe von ganzen bis hin zu durchlaufenden Achtelnoten, dennoch bleibt der gravitätische 3/2-Takt durch die ständige Präsenz von halben Noten erhalten.

Mit rhythmischen Wirkungen stattete Bach auch den dritten Satz, *Allegro*, aus. Der frohe, unkompliziert erscheinende 12/8-Takt wird bereits ab dem dritten Takt durch eigenwillige Synkopenbildungen in den beiden Bratschen gestört. „Gerader" und synkopierter Rhythmus werden miteinander konfrontiert, so dass ein sehr bewegter und die Stimmen miteinander verzahnender Klangeindruck entsteht, der in seiner Dichte dem sehr einfachen Formschema A-B-A entgegengesetzt ist. Aus dem inzwischen wieder vollständigen Orchester exponieren sich die Bratschen durch hohe Lagen, dennoch sind sie nicht Solisten im konzertierenden Sinne, da es hier keinen auffälligen Tutti/Concertino-Kontrast gibt; das sechste Brandenburgische Konzert ist, ebenso wie das dritte, eine „Gemeinschaftsspielmusik".

Ulrike Brenning

Concerto No. 4

Johann Sebastian Bach
(1685–1750)
BWV 1049

I. Allegro

8
Vl. pr.
Fl.
1
2
Vl.
I
II
Vla.
Vc.
Vne.
C.
16
Vl. pr.
Fl.
1
2
Vl.
I
II
Vla.
Vc.
Vne.
C.

23
Vl. pr.
1
Fl.
2
I
Vl.
II
Vla.
Vc.
Vne.
C.
31
Vl. pr.
1
Fl.
2
I
Vl.
II
Vla.
Vc.
Vne.
C.

39
Vl. pr.
1
Fl.
2
I
Vl.
II
Vla.
Vc.
Vne.
C.
46
Vl. pr.
1
Fl.
2
I
Vl.
II
Vla.
Vc.
Vne.
C.

53
Vl. pr.
Fl.
1
2
I
Vl.
II
Vla.
Vc.
Vne.
C.
61
Vl. pr.
Fl.
1
2
I
Vl.
II
Vla.
Vc.
Vne.
C.

70
Vl. pr.
1
Fl.
2
I
Vl.
II
Vla.
Vc.
Vne.
C.
77
Solo

84
Tutti
Vl. pr.
1
Fl.
2
I
Vl.
II
Vla.
Vc.
Vne.
C.
91
Vl. pr.
1
Fl.
2
I
Vl.
II
Vla.
Vc.
Vne.
C.

98
Vl. pr.
1
Fl.
2
I
Vl.
II
Vla.
Vc.
Vne.
C.
105
Vl. pr.
1
Fl.
2
I
Vl.
II
Vla.
Vc.
Vne.
C.

112
Vl. pr.
1
Fl.
2
I
Vl.
II
Vla.
Vc.
Vne.
C.
119
Vl. pr.
1
Fl.
2
I
Vl.
II
Vla.
Vc.
Vne.
C.

126
Vl. pr.
1
Fl.
2
I
Vl.
II
Vla.
Vc.
Vne.
C.
132
Vl. pr.
1
Fl.
2
I
Vl.
II
Vla.
Vc.
Vne.
C.

138
Vl. pr.
1
Fl.
2
I
Vl.
II
Vla.
Vc.
Vne.
C.
145
Vl. pr.
1
Fl.
2
I
Vl.
II
Vla.
Vc.
Vne.
C.

151
Vl. pr.
Fl.
1
2
I
Vl.
II
Vla.
Vc.
Vne.
C.
158
Vl. pr.
Fl.
1
2
I
Vl.
II
Vla.
Vc.
Vne.
C.

165
Vl. pr.
1
Fl.
2
I
Vl.
II
Vla.
Vc.
Vne.
C.
171
1
Fl.
2
Vc.
C.
178
1
Fl.
2
Vc.
C.

184
Vl. pr.
Fl. 1
Fl. 2
Vl. I
Vl. II
Vla.
Vc.
Vne.
C.
tr
189
Vl. pr.
Fl. 1
Fl. 2
Vl. I
Vl. II
Vla.
Vc.
Vne.
C.

193
Vl. pr.
1
Fl.
2
I
Vl.
II
Vla.
Vc.
Vne.
C.
197
Vl. pr.
1
Fl.
2
I
Vl.
II
Vla.
Vc.
Vne.
C.

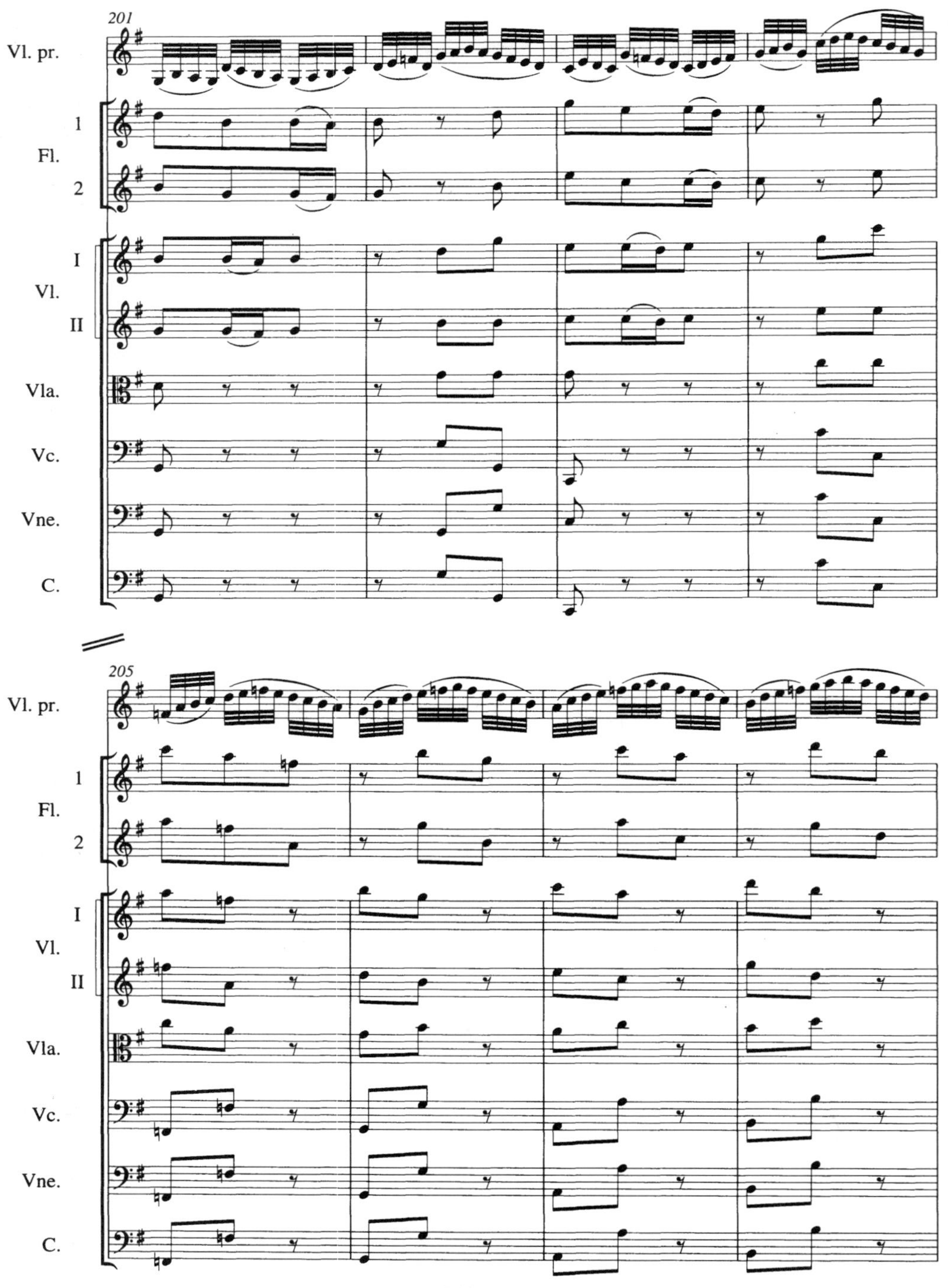
201
Vl. pr.
Fl.
1
2
Vl.
I
II
Vla.
Vc.
Vne.
C.
205

209
Vl. pr.
1
Fl.
2
I
Vl.
II
Vla.
Vc.
Vne.
C.
217
Vl. pr.
1
Fl.
2
I
Vl.
II
Vla.
Vc.
Vne.
C.

224
Vl. pr.
Fl.
1
2
I
Vl.
II
Vla.
Vc.
Vne.
C.
230
Vl. pr.
Fl.
1
2
I
Vl.
II
Vla.
Vc.
Vne.
C.
pp
pp

236
Vl. pr.
1
Fl.
2
I
Vl.
II
Vla.
Vc.
Vne.
C.
242
Vl. pr.
1
Fl.
2
I
Vl.
II
Vla.
Vc.
Vne.
C.

249
Vl. pr.
Fl.
1
2
I
Vl.
II
pp
pp
Vla.
Vc.
Vne.
C.
256
Vl. pr.
Fl.
1
2
I
Vl.
II
Vla.
Vc.
Vne.
C.

263
Vl. pr.
1
Fl.
2
I
Vl.
II
Vla.
Vc.
Vne.
C.
270
Vl. pr.
1
Fl.
2
I
Vl.
II
Vla.
Vc.
Vne.
C.

277
Vl. pr.
1
Fl.
2
I
Vl.
II
Vla.
Vc.
Vne.
C.
284
Vl. pr.
1
Fl.
2
I
Vl.
II
Vla.
Vc.
Vne.
C.

291
Vl. pr.
1
Fl.
2
I
Vl.
II
Vla.
Vc.
Vne.
C.
297
Vl. pr.
1
Fl.
2
I
Vl.
II
Vla.
Vc.
Vne.
C.

303
Vl. pr.
Fl.
1
2
Vl.
I
II
Vla.
Vc.
Vne.
C.
309
tr

315
Vl. pr.
1
Fl.
2
I
Vl.
II
Vla.
Vc.
Vne.
C.
320
Vl. pr.
1
Fl.
2
I
Vl.
II
Vla.
Vc.
Vne.
C.

327
Vl. pr.
Fl.
1
2
Vl.
I
II
Vla.
Vc.
Vne.
C.
333

339
Vl. pr.
1
Fl.
2
I
Vl.
II
Vla.
Vc.
Vne.
C.
346
Vl. pr.
1
Fl.
2
I
Vl.
II
Vla.
Vc.
Vne.
C.

355
Vl. pr.
1
Fl.
2
I
Vl.
II
Vla.
Vc.
Vne.
C.
362
Vl. pr.
1
Fl.
2
I
Vl.
II
Vla.
Vc.
Vne.
C.

368
Vl. pr.
1
Fl.
2
I
Vl.
II
Vla.
Vc.
Vne.
C.
376
Vl. pr.
1
Fl.
2
I
Vl.
II
Vla.
Vc.
Vne.
C.

384
Vl. pr.
Fl.
1
2
Vl.
I
II
Vla.
Vc.
Vne.
C.
391
Vl. pr.
Fl.
1
2
Vl.
I
II
Vla.
Vc.
Vne.
C.

398
Vl. pr.
1
Fl.
2
I
Vl.
II
Vla.
Vc.
Vne.
C.
406
Vl. pr.
1
Fl.
2
I
Vl.
II
Vla.
Vc.
Vne.
C.

414
Vl. pr.
1
Fl.
2
I
Vl.
II
Vla.
Vc.
Vne.
C.
421
Vl. pr.
1
Fl.
2
I
Vl.
II
Vla.
Vc.
Vne.
C.

II. Andante

Violino principale
Flauto [d'Echo] 1 2
Violino [in] ripieno I II
Viola [in] ripien[o]
Violoncello
Violone [in ripieno]
Continuo
7
Vl. pr.
Fl. 1 2
Vl. I II
Vla.
Vc.
Vne.
C.

13
Vl. pr.
Fl.
1
2
f
tr
Vl.
I
II
Vla.
Vc.
Vne.
C.
19
p

25
Vl. pr.
tr
Fl.
1
2
p
Vl.
I
II
Vla.
Vc.
Vne.
C.
30
f
p
f

36
Vl. pr.
1
Fl.
2
I
Vl.
II
Vla.
Vc.
Vne.
C.
tr
42
p

48
Vl. pr.
1
Fl.
2
f
p
f
f
p
f
I
Vl.
II
Vla.
Vc.
Vne.
C.
54
Vl. pr.
tr
1
Fl.
2
tr
tr
p
I
Vl.
II
Vla.
Vc.
Vne.
C.

60
Vl. pr.
Fl.
1
2
Vl.
I
II
Vla.
Vc.
Vne.
C.
p
f
66
tr

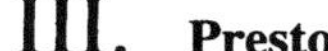

III. Presto

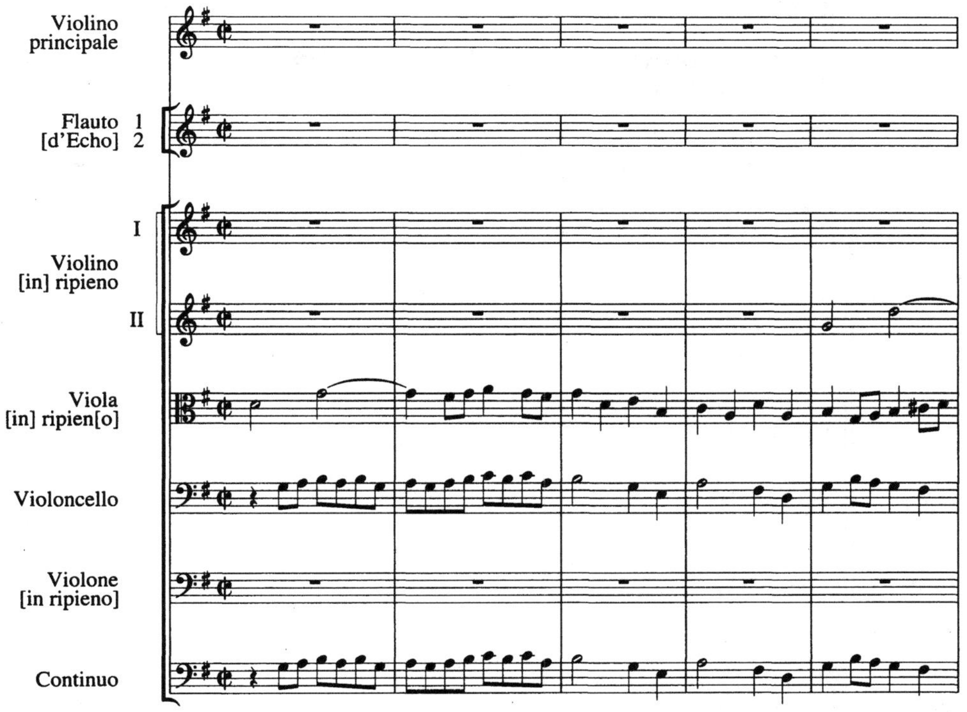
Violino
principale
Flauto 1
[d'Echo] 2
I
Violino
[in] ripieno
II
Viola
[in] ripien[o]
Violoncello
Violone
[in ripieno]
Continuo

6
Vl. pr.
I
Vl.
II
Vla.
Vc.
C.

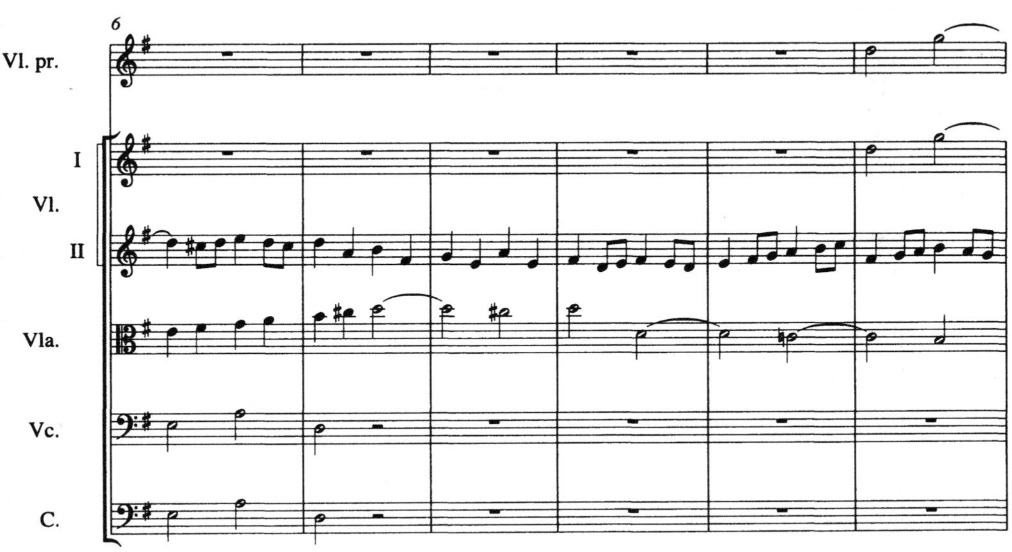

12
Vl. pr.
I
Vl.
II
Vla.
Vc.
Vne.
C.
18
Vl. pr.
Fl. 1 2
a 2
I
Vl.
II
Vla.
Vc.
Vne.
C.

24
Vl. pr.
a 2
Fl. 1 2
I
Vl.
II
Vla.
Vc.
Vne.
C.
29
Vl. pr.
a 2
Fl. 1 2
I
Vl.
II
Vla.
Vc.
Vne.
C.

34
Vl. pr.
a 2
Fl. 1 2
I
Vl.
II
Vla.
Vc.
Vne.
C.
39
Vl. pr.
1
Fl.
2
I
Vl.
II
Vla.
Vc.
Vne.
C.

44
Vl. pr.
1
Fl.
2
49
Vl. pr.
1
Fl.
2
54
Vl. pr.
1
Fl.
2
59
Vl. pr.
1
Fl.
2
Vl. I

64
Vl. pr.
a 2
Fl. 1 2
I
Vl.
II
Vla.
Vc.
Vne.
C.
69
Vl. pr.
a 2
Fl. 1 2
I
Vl.
II
Vla.
Vc.
Vne.
C.

74
Vl. pr.
a 2
Fl. 1 2
I
Vl.
II
Vla.
Vc.
Vne.
C.
78
Vl. pr.
a 2
Fl. 1 2
I
Vl.
II
Vla.
Vc.
Vne.
C.

83
Vl. pr.
a 2
Fl. 1 2
I
Vl.
II
Vla.
Vc.
Vne.
C.
88
Vl. pr.
Vc.
C.
93
Vl. pr.
I
Vl.
II
Vla.
Vc.
Vne.
C.

97
Vl. pr.
1
Fl.
2
I
Vl.
II
Vla.
Vc.
Vne.
C.
101
Vl. pr.
1
Fl.
2
I
Vl.
II
Vla.
Vc.
Vne.
C.

104
Vl. pr.
I
Vl.
II
Vc.
C.
107
Vl. pr.
I
Vl.
II
Vc.
C.
110
Vl. pr.
I
Vl.
II
Vc.
C.

113
Vl. pr.
I
Vl.
II
Vc.
C.
116
Vl. pr.
Vc.
C.
119
Vl. pr.
Vc.
C.

123
Vl. pr.
I
Vl.
II
Vc.
C.
128
Vl. pr.
a 2
Fl. 1 2
I
Vl.
II
Vla.
Vc.
Vne.
C.

133
Vl. pr.
a 2
Fl. 1 2
I
Vl.
II
Vla.
Vc.
Vne.
C.
138
Vl. pr.
a 2
Fl. 1 2
I
Vl.
II
Vla.
Vc.
Vne.
C.

142
Vl. pr.
a 2
Fl. 1 2
I
Vl.
II
Vla.
Vc.
Vne.
C.
146
Vl. pr.
a 2
Fl. 1 2
I
Vl.
II
Vla.
Vc.
Vne.
C.

150
Vl. pr.
1
Fl.
2
I
Vl.
II
Vla.
Vc.
Vne.
C.
155
Vl. pr.
1
Fl.
2
I
Vl.
II
Vla.
Vc.
Vne.
C.

160
1
Fl.
2
Vc.
C.
165
1
Fl.
2
Vc.
C.
170
1
Fl.
2
Vc.
C.

174
Vl. pr.
1
Fl.
2
I
Vl.
II
Vla.
Vc.
Vne.
C.
179
Vl. pr.
1
Fl.
2
I
Vl.
II
Vla.
Vc.
Vne.
C.

184
Vl. pr.
1
Fl.
2
189
Vl. pr.
1
Fl.
2
I
Vl.
II
Vla.
Vc.
Vne.
C.
193
Vl. pr.
1
Fl.
2
I
Vl.
II
Vla.
Vc.
Vne.
C.

198
Vl. pr.
1
Fl.
2
203
Vl. pr.
1
Fl.
2
I
Vl.
II
Vla.
Vc.
Vne.
C.
209
Vl. pr.
a 2
Fl. 1 2
I
Vl.
II
Vla.
Vc.
Vne.
C.

214
Vl. pr.
a 2
Fl. 1 2
I
Vl.
II
Vla.
Vc.
Vne.
C.
219
Vl. pr.
1
Fl.
2
I
Vl.
II
Vla.
Vc.
Vne.
C.

224
Vl. pr.
2
Fl.
1
2
Vl.
I
II
Vla.
Vc.
Vne.
C.
229
Vl. pr.
a 2
Fl.
1
2
Vl.
I
II
Vla.
Vc.
Vne.
C.

235
Vl. pr.
a 2
Fl. 1 2
I
Vl.
II
Vla.
Vc.
Vne.
C.
240
Vl. pr.
a 2
Fl. 1 2
I
Vl.
II
Vla.
Vc.
Vne.
C.

Concerto No. 5

Johann Sebastian Bach
(1685–1750)
BWV 1050

7
Fl.
Vl. pr.
Vl.
Vla.
Vc.
Vne.
C.
10
p
3
EAS 103

13
Fl.
Vl. pr.
Vl.
p
Vla.
Vc.
Vne.
C.
15
Fl.
Vl. pr.
Vl.
Vla.
Vc.
Vne.
C.

17
Fl.
Vl. pr.
Vl.
Vla.
Vc.
Vne.
C.
f
f
f
f
accomp.
♯
6
20
pp
pp
pp
6
6
6
♯

23
Fl.
Vl. pr.
Vl.
Vla.
Vc.
Vne.
C.
26
Fl.
Vl. pr.
Vl.
Vla.
Vc.
Vne.
C.

29
Fl.
Vl. pr.
Vl.
Vla.
Vc.
Vne.
accomp.
C.
p
pp
p
6 6 6 6 6 6 6 6 9 5 6
♯ 5 5 5 ♯ 5
32
Fl.
Vl. pr.
Vl.
pp
Vla.
Vc.
Vne.
C.

35
Fl.
Vl. pr.
Vl.
Vla.
Vc.
Vne.
pp
C.
38
Fl.
Vl. pr.
f
Vl.
f
Vla.
f
Vc.
f
Vne.
f
accomp.
C.

41
Fl.
Vl. pr.
Vl.
Vla.
Vc.
Vne.
C.
44
Fl.
Vl. pr.
Vl.
p
Vla.
p
Vc.
p
Vne.
[p]
C.

46
Fl.
Vl. pr.
Vl.
p
Vla.
p
Vc.
Vne.
C.
3
3
3
3
3
48
Fl.
Vl. pr.
Vl.
Vla.
Vc.
Vne.
C.

50
Fl.
Vl. pr.
Vl.
pp
Vla.
pp
Vc.
p
Vne.
C.
53
Fl.
Vl. pr.
Vl.
Vla.
Vc.
Vne.
C.

56
Fl.
Vl. pr.
Vl.
Vla.
Vc.
Vne.
C.
58
tr
f
accomp.

61
Fl.
Vl. pr.
Vl.
Vla.
Vc.
Vne.
C.
tr
6
5♮
7
5
7
5
64
Fl.
Vl. pr.
Vl.
Vla.
Vc.
Vne.
C.
tr
♯
7
5
7
5

67
Fl.
Vl. pr.
Vl.
Vla.
Vc.
Vne.
C.
70
Fl.
pp
Vl. pr.
pp
Vl.
pp
Vla.
pp
Vc.
pp
Vne.
p
C.

73
Fl.
Vl. pr.
Vl.
Vla.
Vc.
Vne.
C.
76
Fl.
Vl. pr.
Vl.
Vla.
Vc.
Vne.
C.

79
Fl.
Vl. pr.
Vl.
Vla.
Vc.
Vne.
C.
82
Fl.
Vl. pr.
Vl.
Vla.
Vc.
Vne.
C.

85
Fl.
Vl. pr.
Vl.
Vla.
Vc.
Vne.
C.
88
Fl.
Vl. pr.
Vl.
Vla.
Vc.
Vne.
C.

91
Fl.
Vl. pr.
Vl.
Vla.
Vc.
Vne.
C.
94
pp
pp

97
Fl.
Vl. pr.
Vl.
Vla.
Vc.
Vne.
C.
100
Fl.
Vl. pr.
Vl.
Vla.
Vc.
Vne.
accomp.
C.

103
Fl.
Vl. pr.
Vl.
Vla.
Vc.
Vne.
C.
p
p
7
7
7
♯
7
5
7
7
7
7
7
6
5
106
Fl.
Vl. pr.
Vl.
Vla.
Vc.
Vne.
C.
tr
p
p
7
6
7
6
7
6
7
6
7
6

109
Fl.
Vl. pr.
Vl.
Vla.
Vc.
Vne.
p
C.
6
6
3
3
3
112
Fl.
Vl. pr.
Vl.
p
Vla.
p
Vc.
p
Vne.
p
C.
3
3
3

115
Fl.
Vl. pr.
Vl.
Vla.
Vc.
Vne.
C.
117
Fl.
Vl. pr.
Vl.
Vla.
Vc.
Vne.
C.

119
Fl.
Vl. pr.
Vl.
Vla.
Vc.
Vne.
C.
accomp.
122

125
Fl.
Vl. pr.
Vl.
Vla.
Vc.
Vne.
C.
128
Fl.
Vl. pr.
Vl.
Vla.
Vc.
Vne.
C.

131
Fl.
Vl. pr.
Vl.
Vla.
Vc.
Vne.
C.
134
Fl.
Vl. pr.
Vl.
Vla.
Vc.
Vne.
C.
f
f
f
[f]
acc[omp.]
6
5
6

137
Fl.
Vl. pr.
Vl.
Vla.
Vc.
Vne.
C.
p
p
[p]
[p]
6 6 6 6 6
6
5
6 6
6
5
6
5
140
Fl.
Vl. pr.
Vl.
Vla.
Vc.
Vne.
C.

142
Fl.
Vl. pr.
Vl.
Vla.
Vc.
Vne.
C.
144
Fl.
Vl. pr.
Vl.
Vla.
Vc.
Vne.
C.

146
Fl.
Vl. pr.
Vl.
Vla.
Vc.
Vne.
C.
p
p
148
Fl.
Vl. pr.
Vl.
Vla.
Vc.
Vne.
C.

150
Fl.
Vl. pr.
Vl.
Vla.
Vc.
Vne.
C.
152
Fl.
Vl. pr.
Vl.
Vla.
Vc.
Vne.
C.

154
Fl.
Vl. pr.
Vl.
Vla.
Vc.
Vne.
C.
Solo senza stromenti
157
C.
160
163
166
tr

169
172
tr
175
tr
178
tr
181
184
187

190
193
196
198
200
202
6
6
6
6
203

205
207
209
211
213
215
218
Fl.
Vl. pr.
Vl.
Vla.
Vc.
Vne.
C.
accomp.
6
6
6

221
Fl.
Vl. pr.
Vl.
Vla.
Vc.
Vne.
C.
224

II. Affettuoso
Flauto traverso
Violino principale
accomp.
Cembalo
Fl.
Vl. pr.
C.

13
Fl.
Vl. pr.
C.
p
16
p
19
f
[f]
tr
22
tr
[p]

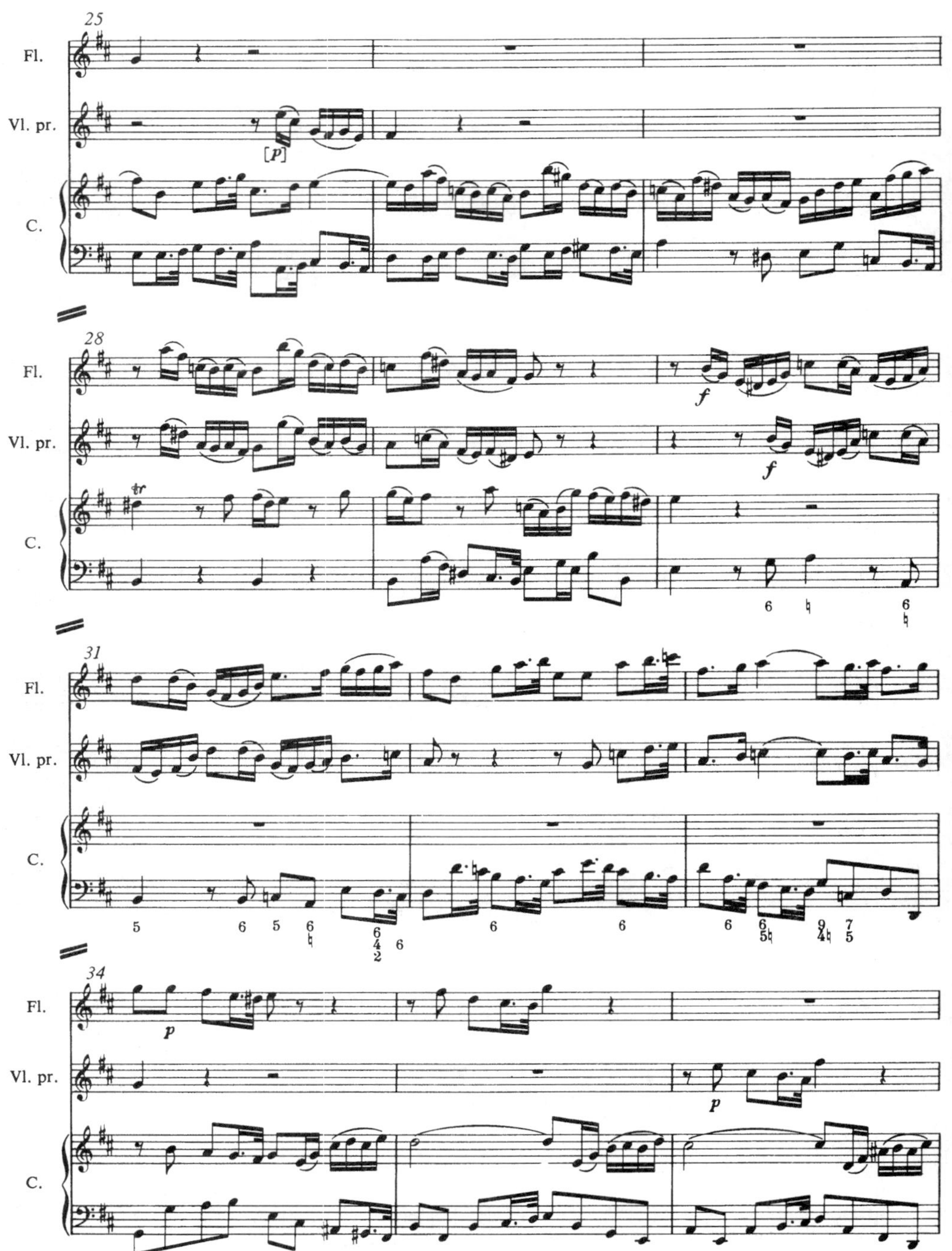
25
Fl.
Vl. pr.
[p]
C.
28
Fl.
f
Vl. pr.
f
C.
31
Fl.
Vl. pr.
C.
34
Fl.
p
Vl. pr.
p
C.

37
Fl.
Vl. pr.
C.
40
Fl.
Vl. pr.
C.
43
Fl.
Vl. pr.
C.
f
f
46
Fl.
Vl. pr.
C.

III. Allegro
Flauto traverso
Violino principale
Violino in ripieno
Viola in ripieno
Violoncello
Violone
Cembalo concertato
8
Fl.
Vl. pr.
C.
7 5 5 6
15
Fl.
Vl. pr.
C.
tr
tr

21
Fl.
Vl. pr.
C.
27
Fl.
Vl. pr.
Vl.
Vla.
Vc.
Vne.
accomp.
C.
34
Fl.
Vl. pr.
Vl.
Vla.
Vc.
Vne.
C.

42
Fl.
Vl. pr.
Vl.
Vla.
Vc.
Vne.
C.
46
Fl.
Vl. pr.
Vl.
Vla.
Vc.
Vne.
C.

51
Fl.
Vl. pr.
Vl.
Vla.
Vc.
Vne.
C.
58
Fl.
Vl. pr.
Vl.
Vla.
Vc.
Vne.
C.

62
Fl.
Vl. pr.
Vl.
Vla.
Vc.
Vne.
accomp.
C.
69
acc [omp.]

76
Fl.
Vl. pr.
Vl.
Vla.
Vc.
Vne.
C.
p
6
5
6
5
83
Solo
f
pp
6
6
6
7
6
5
4

90
Fl.
Vl. pr.
Vl.
Vla.
Vc.
Vne.
C.
97
Fl.
Vl. pr.
p
Solo
Vl.
f
pp
Vla.
Vc.
Vne.
C.
6
6
7
6
♯
4
5+
♯
6

104
Fl.
Vl. pr.
Vl.
Vla.
Vc.
Vne.
C.
111
118

125
Fl.
Vl. pr.
Vl.
Vla.
Vc.
Vne.
accomp.
C.
131
Fl.
Vl. pr.
Vl.
Vla.
Vc.
Vne.
C.

138
Fl.
Vl. pr.
Vl.
Vla.
Vc.
Vne.
C.
5 6 5 8 5+ 6 5 6 4+ 2 6 6 5 6 4 #
144
Fl.
Vl. pr.
Vl.
Vla.
Vc.
Vne.
C.
tr
p
cantabile
5 6 6 5 7 # # 6 4+ 6 6 6 4 5 #

150
Fl.
Vl. pr.
Vl.
Vla.
Vc.
Vne.
C.
157
[p]
p
tr
164

170
C.
176
Fl.
Vl. pr.
Vl.
Vla.
Vc.
Vne.
C.
183
Fl.
Vl. pr.
Vl.
Vla.
Vc.
Vne.
C.

190
Fl.
Vl. pr.
Vl.
Vla.
Vc.
Vne.
C.
196
Fl.
Vl. pr.
Vl.
Vla.
Vc.
Vne.
C.

202
Fl.
Vl. pr.
Vl.
Vla.
Vc.
Vne.
C.
208
Fl.
Vl. pr.
Vl.
Vla.
Vc.
Vne.
C.

214
Fl.
Vl. pr.
Vl.
Vla.
Vc.
Vne.
C.
tasto solo
221
Fl.
Vl. pr.
Vl.
Vla.
Vc.
Vne.
accomp.
C.

227
Fl.
Vl. pr.
Vl.
Vla.
Vc.
Vne.
C.
234
Fl.
Vl. pr.
C.
241
Fl.
Vl. pr.
C.

247
Fl.
Vl. pr.
C.
252
Fl.
Vl. pr.
C.
258
Fl.
Vl. pr.
Vl.
Vla.
Vc.
Vne.
C.
accomp.

263
Fl.
Vl. pr.
Vl.
Vla.
Vc.
Vne.
C.
6
6
5
6
6
6
6
5
6
5
270
Fl.
Vl. pr.
Vl.
Vla.
Vc.
Vne.
C.

276
Fl.
Vl. pr.
Vl.
Vla.
Vc.
Vne.
C.
280
Fl.
Vl. pr.
Vl.
Vla.
Vc.
Vne.
C.

286
Fl.
Vl. pr.
Vl.
Vla.
Vc.
Vne.
C.
tr
292
accomp.
6

297
Fl.
Vl. pr.
Vl.
Vla.
Vc.
Vne.
C.
304
acc[omp.]

Concerto No. 6

Johann Sebastian Bach
(1685–1750)
BWV 1051

I. Allegro

6
Vla.
da br.
1
2
Vla.
da gba.
1
2
Vc.
V. e C.
9
12

15
1
Vla.
da br.
2
1
Vla.
da gba.
2
Vc.
V. e C.
18
1
Vla.
da br.
2
1
Vla.
da gba.
2
Vc.
V. e C.
21
1
Vla.
da br.
2
1
Vla.
da gba.
2
Vc.
V. e C.

24
Vla.
da br.
1
2
Vla.
da gba.
1
2
Vc.
V. e C.
27
30

33
Vla.
da br.
1
2
Vla.
da gba.
1
2
Vc.
V. e C.
36
39
p

42
Vla.
da br.
Vla.
da gba.
Vc.
V. e C.
45
f
48

51
Vla.
da br.
1
2
Vla.
da gba.
1
2
Vc.
V. e C.
p
54
f
57

60
Vla. da br. 1 2
Vla. da gba. 1 2
Vc.
V. e C.
63
66

69
Vla. da br.
1
2
Vla. da gba.
1
2
Vc.
V. e C.
72
75

78
Vla.
da br.
1
2
Vla.
da gba.
1
2
Vc.
V. e C.
81
84
p
[p]
f

87
Vla.
da br.
1
2
Vla.
da gba.
1
2
Vc.
V. e C.
90
93

96
Vla.
da br.
Vla.
da gba.
Vc.
V. e C.
99
Vla.
da br.
Vla.
da gba.
Vc.
V. e C.
102
Vla.
da br.
Vla.
da gba.
Vc.
V. e C.

105
Vla.
da br.
1
2
Vla.
da gba.
1
2
Vc.
V. e C.
108
111

114
Vla. da br.
1
2
Vla. da gba.
1
2
Vc.
V. e C.
117
120

123
Vla.
da br.
Vla.
da gba.
Vc.
V. e C.
125
128

II. Adagio ma non tanto
Viola da braccio
Viola da gamba
Violoncello
Violone e Cembalo
Vla. da br.
Vla. da gba.
Vc.
V. e. C.
tr

12
Vla.
da br.
Vla.
da gba.
Vc.
V. e C.
15
19

23
Vla. da br.
1
2
Vla. da gba.
1
2
Vc.
V. e C.
26
29
tr

33
Vla.
da br.
Vla.
da gba.
Vc.
V. e C.
36
Vla.
da br.
Vla.
da gba.
Vc.
V. e C.
39
Vla.
da br.
Vla.
da gba.
Vc.
V. e C.

42
Vla.
da br.
Vla.
da gba.
Vc.
V. e C.
tr
45
48

51
Vla.
da br.
Vla.
da gba.
Vc.
V. e C.
55
59
tr
p
f

III. Allegro

Viola
da braccio
1
2
Viola
da gamba
1
2
Violoncello
Violone
e Cembalo
4
Vla.
da br.
Vla.
da gba.
Vc.
V. e C.
8

11
Vla. da br. 1
2
Vla. da gba. 1
2
Vc.
V. e C.
13
16

18
Vla.
da br.
1
2
Vla.
da gba.
1
2
Vc.
V. e C.
20
22
tr

24
Vla.
da br.
Vla.
da gba.
Vc.
V. e C.
26
Vla.
da br.
Vla.
ia gba.
Vc.
V. e C.
28
Vla.
da br.
Vla.
da gba.
Vc.
V. e C.

30
Vla.
da br.
1
2
Vla.
da gba.
1
2
Vc.
V. e C.
32
34

36
Vla. da br.
1
2
Vla. da gba.
1
2
Vc.
V. e C.
38
Vla. da br.
1
2
Vla. da gba.
1
2
Vc.
V. e C.
42
Vla. da br.
1
2
Vla. da gba.
1
2
Vc.
V. e C.

46
Vla.
da br.
Vla.
da gba.
Vc.
V. e C.
48
50

52
Vla.
da br.
1
2
Vla.
da gba.
1
2
Vc.
V. e C.
55
57

59
Vla. da br.
1
2
Vla. da gba.
1
2
Vc.
V. e C.
61
63
tr
tr

66
Vla.
da br.
1
2
Vla.
da gba.
1
2
Vc.
V.e C.
70
Vla.
da br.
1
2
Vla.
da gba.
1
2
Vc.
V.e C.
74
Vla.
da br.
1
2
Vla.
da gba.
1
2
Vc.
V.e C.

76
Vla.
da br.
Vla.
da gba.
Vc.
V.e C.
78
81

83
Vla.
da br.
1
2
Vla.
da gba.
1
2
Vc.
V. e C.
86
tr
88

90
Vla. da br.
1
2
Vla. da gba.
1
2
Vc.
V. e C.
92
94

96
Vla.
da br.
1
2
Vla.
da gba.
1
2
Vc.
V. e C.
98
100

102
1
Vla.
da br.
2
1
Vla.
da gba.
2
Vc.
V. e C.
105
108
tr